CW00672143

SCANDI **RUSTIC**

SCANDI RUSTIC

CREATING A COZY & HAPPY HOME

REBECCA LAWSON
& REENA SIMON

PHOTOGRAPHY BY
BENJAMIN EDWARDS

RYLAND PETERS & SMALL
LONDON • NEW YORK

Art director
Leslie Harrington

Senior designer
Megan Smith

**Senior commissioning
editor** Annabel Morgan

Location research
Jess Walton

Head of production
Patricia Harrington

Editorial director
Julia Charles

Publisher
Cindy Richards

Indexer
Hilary Bird

First published in 2020 by
Ryland Peters & Small
20–21 Jockey's Fields,
London WC1R 4BW
and
341 E 116th St
New York, NY 10029
www.rylandpeters.com

Text © Rebecca Lawson and
Reena Simon 2020
Design and photographs ©
Ryland Peters & Small 2020

ISBN 978-1-78879-246-2

Printed and bound in China

10 9 8 7 6 5

The authors' moral rights have
been asserted. All rights
reserved. No part of this
publication may be reproduced,
stored in a retrieval system or
transmitted in any form or
by any means, electronic,
mechanical, photocopying or
otherwise, without the prior
permission of the publisher.

A CIP record for this
book is available from the British
Library. US Library of Congress
Cataloging-in-Publication Data
has been applied for.

MIX
Paper from
responsible sources
FSC® C106563
FSC
www.fsc.org

Contents

Introduction

Some friends meet at school, others at university or through mutual friends. However, it was Instagram that brought us together in 2016. We were both on maternity leave at the time while renovating our first family homes (in London and Cardiff) and we quickly discovered a shared love of Scandinavian design and living.

Over the last four years, we have carved out careers as award-winning bloggers and social media content creators with a love of rustic, Scandinavian-style interiors with a cozy feel. Our focus is on creating a home that contains the traditional, pared-back elements of Scandinavian design alongside plenty of rustic natural materials and textures for an end result that's homely, relaxed and inviting.

When writing this book, we wanted to share the Scandi Rustic style that we love, so we visited homes across Scandinavia and the UK that reflect this style in subtly different ways. What each of the homes shares is a feeling of coziness and warmth that nurtures a sense of wellbeing and contentment. And now more than ever our homes are our sanctuaries — the places we retreat to for comfort and calm.

We hope you enjoy coming on this journey with us. The experience has truly inspired us both as we prepare to embark on our next renovation projects.

Reena and Rebecca

AT ONE WITH NATURE
Creating a strong connection with nature and opting for simple, pared-down designs are two key elements of Scandinavian interiors. The home of Mette and Masahiro, nestled in the Danish countryside, showcases this understated approach perfectly (opposite).

SHINE A LIGHT
Light – both natural and artificial – has a starring role to play in Scandi-style interiors. Here, the setting sun casts soft shadows in the hallway of Lisa Brass's home on the West Sussex coast (above).

Scandinavian inspirations

Creating a cozy home

The Danish concept of *hygge* translates as finding coziness and contentment through the simple things in life. Many Scandinavians treat their homes as a *hygge* retreat and would rather spend time at home than anywhere else. Embracing the simple pleasures in life, as our Scandinavian friends do, is to feel happy. Creating a cozy living environment is centred around establishing a connection with your home and everything in it, creating a warm atmosphere and experience that you can enjoy with friends and family.

When we travelled to Scandinavia to photograph the homes featured in this book, we were struck by the feeling of intimacy and comfort that the homeowners had created. On the following pages, we share tips and ideas that will help you to create Scandi Rustic style in your own home. We'll walk you through the key elements of the look, from choosing a colour palette and the right lighting to adding in textiles and other textures, as well as finding the finishing touches that will bring interest to your home while reflecting your own personality and interests. After that, join us as we visit an array of beautiful Scandi Rustic homes – we are sure that they will inspire you just as they have inspired us.

A HAPPY HOME

Every home needs a *hygge* spot for comfort and relaxation. Plan a snug nook where you can grab a cup of coffee and escape for five minutes' peace (this page and opposite), or a deep sofa where you can put your feet up in front of the wood-burning stove with family and friends (right).

SCANDI **RUSTIC**
Elements

COLOUR

The colours we surround ourselves with in our homes can have a powerful impact on our state of mind. Colour, and the way that we experience it, can subtly alter our moods both positively and negatively. A carefully chosen palette can have a beneficial effect on our health and happiness, evoking feelings of contentment and creating calm.

Scandinavian interiors are synonymous with neutral colour schemes and minimalist, monochrome decor. However, this is just one aspect of Scandinavian design, and the homes we have featured in this book demonstrate the breadth of colours and tones that can be used to create a cozy Nordic-inspired home. In these homes, the owners have made subtly different colour choices, each drawing upon hues that create a warm and inviting atmosphere.

Calming shades of white and grey, natural hues such as blush, terracotta and linen and darker, earthier tones including green, blue and rust are all suited to a Scandi Rustic home. The key is to understand how these different colours make you feel, then to match those feelings to the different spaces in your home.

For example, in the bedroom of Mike and Kate Lawley, neutral shades have been used to create a peaceful space that invites rest and relaxation (opposite). The soft white walls are cool and quiet, while earthier accents produce feelings of stability and comfort. The colours on the walls, the textiles on the bed and the wooden floor all harmonize. Interconnected layers of colour, texture and light have been woven together to create a cohesive scheme.

While there are no hard and fast rules about how many different colours you should use in your home, a scheme tends to work most successfully where three or four key shades are chosen and then repeated to create a sense of rhythm, continuity and flow.

SUBTLE SHADES
A display in a small nook at the Swedish farmhouse home of Anna Kubel shows how the brightest whites can combine with softer natural tones and dark hues to create a *hygge* home.

Light and bright

R81A
X48
Gentle Lamb
Goose Feather
R75A
W47A
X37
White Cliffs
W13E
Wedding Cake
Fluffy Robe
L8A
Tahitian Vanilla
W43E
Wispy White

A pale, bleached colour palette is the one most commonly associated with Scandinavian interiors.

Tranquil, soft tones of white and grey tend to be popular in the Nordic region because they reflect natural light and maximize sunlight, which is in short supply during the long, dark Scandinavian winters. An all-white scheme can offer a fresh, crisp and clean feel to any room, but to prevent the space from feeling clinical or cold it's essential to incorporate layers of texture and depth of shade.

The Danish home of Pernille Grønkjær Taatø (above left) is a perfect example of how white can be used to create a restful and light-filled home. Douglas Fir floors and whitewashed beams and walls open up the interior, while the black wall lights provide contrast and throw a wash of warm light (above left). Pernille has mixed the clean lines of her contemporary kitchen with the organic outlines of vintage ceramics and driftwood foraged from local beaches. You can recreate this effect and add texture and warmth to an all-white space with sheepskins, rugs and natural linen cushions and throws (left and opposite).

Soft and natural

Using colour to create a connection with nature will bring the outdoors in and enhance a sense of wellbeing.

Earthy tones drawn from the natural world such as terracotta, flax and clay can help to create a relaxed rustic interior. And choosing a subtle, natural colour scheme is a good way to introduce colour into your home without it feeling overwhelming.

In the bedroom of interior stylist and photographer Anna Kubel, limewashed walls mimic the look and feel of raw plaster while linen bedding in shades of pink fall upon floorboards stripped back to their natural state (left). This is a gentle, romantic room with a strong connection to the Swedish countryside beyond the window.

The kitchen was one of our favourite spaces in the home of stylist Kay Prestney, where raw plastered walls finished with a coat of varnish provide a subtle blush-pink backdrop to Kay's eclectic and much loved collection of handmade ceramics (left). Her shelves were made from old scaffold planks teamed with modern brackets and given a rustic, gently aged appearance with the use of a brass chalk paint.

Dark and moody

Inky black, charcoal grey, midnight blue and earthy shades of brown all form part of an alluring rustic palette.

Dark colours may not be immediately associated with cozy comfort, but when balanced with lighter colours and juxtaposed with plenty of appealing textures, these rich hues bring rooms weight and depth and feel cocooning. The cloakroom in Lisa Brass's home is a case in point (opposite). The room has been clad in tongue and groove panelling and painted jet black. This may seem a bold choice for a small room, but the space doesn't feel gloomy. Instead, the dark walls play on the room's snug character and act as the perfect backdrop for assorted baskets, fresh foliage from the garden displayed in an earthenware vase and soft textiles in the shape of hanging coats.

If using dark colours feels daunting, then choosing furniture and accessories in deep, moody hues to set against light walls may feel easier. A wooden headboard made from blackened wood sits against pale walls in the bedroom of Mike and Kate Lawley, adding a note of richness and intensity without overwhelming the space (below left).

LIGHTING

Good lighting is one of the most fundamental elements of a Scandi Rustic home. It creates the right atmosphere and sets the mood for a successful and inviting living space.

In Scandinavia the winter months are long and dark and the focus for many homeowners is on maximizing natural daylight. We were mesmerized by the way the oversized windows allowed light to stream into Masahiro and Mette's home in Denmark, casting atmospheric shadows across the timber-clad walls and ceiling (opposite). Rooflights are also a popular choice for many Scandinavian homes, as they allow more light to flow in and provide views of the sky.

Making the most of daylight is important, but artificial lighting is essential – it keeps homes feeling warm and cheerful and illuminates our daily activities throughout the winter months, when daylight is in short supply and the nights are long. If you are approaching the renovation of a house or even building your own home from scratch, it is crucial to incorporate a lighting scheme into your plans from the outset and not just as an afterthought.

The starting point for effective lighting is to have your interior and exterior floorplans ready. You can then work your way through your home thinking about the different purposes of each room, the moods you want to create and how the lighting will bring each space to life.

Bear in mind that each room will need more than one source of light and should include three or even four layers of ambient, statement and task lighting. By layering light fittings in this way, you will create a lighting scheme that ticks all the boxes: cozy, aesthetically pleasing and functional. Finally, don't forget that all mains lighting should be installed with dimmer switches to ensure maximum flexibility.

PLEASING THE EYE
For a snug, intimate home, lighting is required at eye level as well as overhead. We loved the way that homeowner Elin Wallin has played with the height of her decorative pendant light, hanging it low to illuminate the kitchen counter.

Cozy Lighting

Create a cozy ambient lighting scheme using natural light sources like flames and candlelight combined with dimmable lamps for a laidback, restful mood.

Is there anything more calming than sitting watching the flames of a roaring fire or flickering candlelight? These are both indispensable sources of light for a Scandi Rustic home. We both love candlelight, and not just in the evening when the sun has gone down. By day it also creates a tranquil and peaceful mood.

When it comes to electric light, a combination of a pendant plus wall lights and table or floor lamps will create a more soothing and atmospheric effect than a single overhead fixture. Combining several different light sources will create scattered pockets of light that enliven a room. Pick your bulbs wisely and opt for ones that cast a soft, warm and relaxing light rather than a cool white one.

Statement lighting

A statement light can transform the aesthetic of a room from ordinary to spectacular. However, 'statement' does not necessarily mean oversized. Simple pendants can have equal impact.

Statement lights come in many forms, shapes and designs but they have one thing in common – they all have as much impact when switched off as when they are on. Think of such a fitting as a piece of furniture that will complement or contrast with the other materials and objects in a room to bring a scheme together. For example, an oversized rattan shade works really well as a contrast with the smooth grey concrete walls at The Hide (above left). If your decorative style is more low key, try something smaller, like the dainty pleated pendant in Anna Kubel's home, and hang it low to place emphasis on the design (opposite above right).

For dramatic effect, go for a statement light hung low over a kitchen island or dining table. In the home of lighting designer Tom Raffield, a steam-bent hoop of solid oak with suspended filament bulbs reinvents the chandelier and becomes a focal point for the room adding a striking feature (opposite).

Functional lighting

Lighting designer Tom Raffield sums it up perfectly when he says 'every piece of lighting must be beautiful in form and practical in function.'

Functional or task lighting is an important part of any scheme, illuminating the activities you wish to carry out in a particular area. There are a range of different choices in this category, including pendant lights, spotlights and adjustable wall and desk lights. In Lisa Brass's kitchen, pendants illuminate the sink (opposite), while a bedside lamp has a moveable arm for maximum flexibility (above). To add a luxe edge to task lighting, look for fixtures made from brass, copper or brushed nickel, such as these wall lights in the home of Mike and Kate Lawley (above right) Outdoor lighting also has a role to play, making make your home look inviting and well lit, as with these utility style wall lights at Island Cottage (above left).

TEXTURE

A Scandi Rustic home takes a considered approach to choosing textures, from the wall finishes to flooring to soft furnishings and decorative objects. Fluid fabrics such as linen are juxtaposed with unyielding materials like concrete or stone to create contrast and visual interest.

Texture is all about creating a pleasing sensory experience in your home, and combining a variety of contrasting finishes will create a relaxed, welcoming atmosphere. Tactile natural materials are layered together seamlessly in Anna Kubel's Swedish farmhouse (opposite). In the light-filled sunroom, a curvy rattan sofa sits on whitewashed wooden floors, the seat piled with linen cushions and throws. We could spend hours sitting here, drinking coffee and gazing through misted windows at the ponies grazing in the fields beyond.

Linen is a textile we saw in abundance in all the homes featured in this book. Made from the plant flax, it is a natural and eco-friendly fabric, sturdy and durable, with an appearance that improves with age and washing. Its coarse surface and crumpled appearance make it a great choice for adding a lived-in feel to an interior.

Cushions, sheepskins and blankets will all add valuable texture to a room, but think of including other elements such as rugs. You can create contrast by pairing a wool or cotton rug with one made from natural fibres such as jute, or try layering them up for a truly cozy feel.

Plants and foliage add another layer of texture. Anna Kubel uses her sunroom to propagate new plants and it was soothing to be surrounded by her plants in their aged terracotta and earthenware pots. Embracing the imperfect by prizing simple objects or those with a patina that has developed over time is at the heart of the Japanese philosophy of wabi-sabi, which has traits similar to those found in Scandinavian design.

RECLAIMED SURFACES
In Susan Mogensen's home, the kitchen floor is made of reclaimed brick – a material more usually associated with the outdoors. The worn brick works perfectly here, teamed with a soft, deep-pile sheepskin that's been casually draped over the bench beside a wooden dining table.

Layering textiles

Layering with textiles such as throws, blankets and rugs is a key component of Scandi design and often centres around a neutral, earthy or muted colour palette.

Textiles will work hard to soften and warm up hard surfaces such as concrete or stone. Build layers of textiles into a room from the ground up, combining different fabrics and textures to make an inviting space full of depth and detail. Elin Wallin's daughter's room is a great example of how to use textiles to create a dreamy sleep space (opposite). The layered linen bedding can be changed with the seasons and Elin has used sheer cream cotton to create a canopy that's suspended from the ceiling above the bed. The effect is quite magical — imagine falling asleep each night under the cloud-like drapes and dreaming of adventures yet to come.

MATERIALS

The Scandinavian landscape is a mesmerizing mix of long coastlines, mountains, glimmering lakes and shady forests. The timber-clad houses mirror this landscape and blend into their surroundings, designed to defy long hours of darkness and harsh winter weather.

Older, more traditional homes tend to have horizontal cladding (often stained or painted red) and large windows with few glazing bars to maximize natural daylight. These are places to hunker down through the long, cold winter months with the fire or stove lit and candles flickering.

Over the last century, Scandinavian architecture has changed. It still makes use of traditional materials such as timber and stone, but has a fresher, more modernist-inspired feel. Vertical Siberian larch cladding is often used, but with slim profile boards narrowly spaced and left unstained to fade to a beautiful silvery grey that mirrors the bleak winter skies. Ancient techniques developed in Japan to char wood and make it weatherproof are also popular here.

This approach is also apparent in the UK. The exterior of Island Cottage on the windswept West Sussex coast looks like a traditional flint cottage from the front, but at the rear it has been extended and covered in beautiful larch cladding, so it seamlessly blends in with the surrounding nature reserve.

When it comes to making choices for an interior scheme, natural materials, simplicity, comfort, texture and tactility should be the guiding principles. Using a consistent palette of materials throughout a home will create a sense of flow and tranquillity. Polished concrete or wooden floors can feel more modern than carpets in living and sleeping spaces and introduce valuable texture. On the walls, consider using lime-based paints, micro-cement or plaster for chalky, nuanced finishes that only get better with age.

SUBTLE CONTRASTS
Interior stylist Kay Prestney has used raw plaster on both walls and ceilings throughout her home. In the hallway, its soft pastel tones on the ceiling combine with clean white walls to provide a gentle backdrop to a treasured collection of baskets and other vintage finds.

Inside and out

With over two-thirds of Scandinavia covered in forest, timber is an abundant and frequently used material for both exterior and interior finishes.

The Danish home of Mette and Masahiro is the perfect example of how Scandinavian architecture uses natural materials to blend buildings with the surrounding landscape (opposite). The couple chose cedar boards treated with the Japanese Shou Sugi Ban technique — a method used to preserve wood by charring it with fire. In Cornwall, cedar shingles faded to grey by the Cornish weather blend The Hide into adjoining woodland (above and above right). Layering reclaimed materials into the interior architecture of your home, as in this Danish kitchen, is a sustainable way to add character. The herringbone brick floor may look centuries old, but it was laid as part of a recent renovation using salvaged bricks (above left).

FINISHING TOUCHES

It's the finishing touches that make an interior into a home. This is where you have to follow your instincts, choosing pieces that add soul and your story to a space.

Both of us have spent many a happy hour searching for and sourcing accessories for our homes, from books, art and favourite photographs that tell a story or hold memories to candles, mirrors and vintage pieces that are worn with time. And don't forget plants and fresh flowers – with their natural scents, shapes and colours, they can transform the feeling of a space by lifting your emotions.

Open shelving offers a great opportunity for displaying such objects. Tom and Danielle Raffield have carefully curated pieces arranged on their kitchen shelving (opposite). The layering of materials in this room sees polished concrete juxtaposed with black-stained wood, and the trailing plants, favoured objects and gleam of metal on the shelves enliven these hard surfaces. We loved the medicinal brown bottles with soap decanted into them and the handmade chopping boards in varying sizes stacked against the concrete splashback. The use of blush pink as an accent colour is picked up here in the shade of the ceramic mugs. The subtle hue recurs throughout the couple's home to soften the effect of the natural timber that has a presence on every wall and ceiling. Using accessories to introduce an element of colour is a great way to add personality to a neutral home.

It has been said that nothing is finished in an interior without art, but it can also be the starting point for an entire decorative scheme – pick out a colour or shape from a beloved artwork and use that as inspiration. What you chose to hang on your walls is one of the most personal choices in a home.

IN THE MIX
Decorative accessories such as cushions, plants, vases and art allow you to introduce colour or to refresh an interior without too much work or investment. At The Hide, a bolthole deep in the Cornish countryside, a terracotta pot housing a feathery houseplant stands out against all the grey tones while the fringed linen cushion cozies up this minimalist space.

All in the detail

It was the finishing touches added to the Scandi Rustic homes we visited that expressed the individuality of the owners, allowing it to shine through.

Smaller items work well on open shelves, where they can be admired close up. In the home of stylist Elin Wallin, her String shelving system – a Scandinavian classic – displays books and magazines alongside quirky vintage pieces (opposite above left). Glossy red winter berries add a note of colour.

One-off vintage finds bring character to any home. Many years of rummaging at salvage yards and car boot sales means that Kay Prestney's home is full of such treasures. In daughter Bella's room, a letter 'B' rescued from an old sign sits alongside pens in a ceramic pot (opposite below). At Island Cottage, vintage bottles are used to show off natural finds collected on walks in the surrounding nature reserve (left).

Finishing touches are a good way to add contrasting texture. In Tom and Dani Raffield's home, a steam-bent wooden shelf of their own design sits against ancient stone walls (centre), while at Island Cottage indulgent bedding softens limewashed walls (above left).

SCANDI **RUSTIC**
Homes

INDUSTRIAL RUSTIC

This converted Victorian schoolhouse full of charming original features and with sprawling views over Wiltshire's Box Valley has an unexpectedly rustic interior that is cozy and welcoming.

Wiltshire-based couple Mike Read and Kate Lawley have worked tirelessly over the past few years to convert a Victorian schoolhouse into a home that is a peaceful haven designed to nurture all five senses.

When they first viewed the house back in 2016, the couple had been searching without success for a period renovation project. As soon as they saw the unusual mezzanine layout and soaring ceilings of the old schoolhouse, they knew they had found their project. Although the property was in a poor state of repair, they were confident they could turn it into the warehouse-style space they had always dreamed of.

The property is set on a hill and the front door is at the back of the building. The house is entered on a mezzanine level from which the bedrooms lead off. When Mike and Kate first viewed the house, the kitchen was located on this level, but their architect, Nicole du Pisanie of Stonewood Design, inspired them to rethink the space and create one large open-plan living area downstairs. Now when you enter, the huge original arched windows offer uninterrupted views over the rolling Wiltshire countryside. It is this connection to the outdoors that makes the house feel so spacious. When we visited we were struck by a sense of calmness. The

scent of candles filled the air, with gently dimmed lights and soft background music making for an extremely inviting home.

Mike and Kate wanted to reclaim, restore and repurpose as many elements in the existing fabric of the building as possible, and carried out much of the renovation work themselves with the help of Kate's father, who is a talented carpenter. The couple lived with Kate's parents during the renovation, returning from work and heading straight to the schoolhouse to spend long evenings working on the project. They even taught themselves many of the skills needed to complete the project. After watching tutorials on YouTube, Mike tackled the task of making the concrete countertop for the huge island unit that forms the heart of the kitchen. Made off-site in a friend's garden, it is so large that it took eight people to carry it into the house when it was fitted. It's wonderful handcrafted items such as the countertop that make this such a personal home full of character.

The dramatic open staircase is the focal point of the home, dividing the open-plan downstairs space into different areas. The couple designed it themselves and used a local company to manufacture the steel spine, which was then installed by Kate's dad.

RAW AND RECLAIMED

At the heart of the couple's open-plan living space is a large kitchen island clad in reclaimed wood with a smooth concrete countertop made by Mike. The island unit serves as a natural gathering point, with rattan bar stools adding texture and offering an inviting place to sit. The kitchen units were sourced secondhand from eBay and painted white to create a calm backdrop that allows the other textures in the kitchen to take centre stage.

It can be a challenge to make a large open-plan space feel intimate but Mike and Kate have achieved this with the use of different types of wood that range in colour, age, grain and finish. The contrast of the worn 200-year-old floorboards with the sleek contemporary wooden dining table adds warmth and visual interest. The restricted colour palette typical of Scandinavian interiors has been brought to life through the addition of varied textiles, patterned cushions, layered rugs and a scattering of houseplants plus handpicked Scandi luxe items from the couple's favourite sources. Wicker, raw plaster finishes, reclaimed wood and steel have been used throughout, giving the interior a sense of consistency and flow.

The lighting has been well thought out, and is used as an architectural feature to frame different aspects and draw the eye to specific objects. We both fell in love with the Hay Marble pendant light suspended from the double-height ceiling of the living room. In the kitchen area, the metallic gleam of the brushed brass wall lights soften the raw plaster finish on the walls.

The novice renovators have achieved an incredible amount in a short space of time and work on the house continues, albeit at a slower pace. They are currently finishing a utility room and downstairs shower in rooms that lead off the kitchen, further employing their newly-acquired concreting skills to create a huge concrete sink for the space. Upstairs, there is still another floor to complete which, when finished, will provide an additional bedroom and bathroom with stunning views over the beautiful Box Valley.

LOFT-STYLE LIVING

As part of the renovation of the property the kitchen was relocated downstairs to create a spacious interconnected kitchen/living space with a double-height ceiling. The open-plan living area has the warehouse/loft feel that Mike and Kate were aiming for, but the use of reclaimed materials, soft lighting and layered textures means it is also a warm, cozy environment. In winter, the couple curl up on the sofa under throws and light their contemporary black wood-burning stove, which sits in a corner of the living room (above).

SEPARATION OF SPACES

The open-plan living area is divided into separate relaxing, living and dining areas by an open timber staircase that was designed by the couple and built by Kate's father. The chunky wooden treads and dark metal frame echo materials used elsewhere in the building. The staircase adds an industrial edge to the interior of the old schoolhouse, and this is further enhanced by the large Crittall-style metal-framed internal window of the master bedroom, which overlooks this area.

SOFT LAYERS
In the bedroom, throws and cushions in cotton, wool and linen soften the unscreened windows and the imposing feel of the thick old stone walls

CONNECTION WITH NATURE
The bedroom walls are neutral, but textiles and accessories introduce earthy accents of ochre, moss and flax. These add warmth and echo the colours of the Wiltshire hills, which are framed by the original arched windows. Vintage glass bottles and vases filled with dried grasses, twigs and leaves create a further connection with nature.

CREATING A *HYGGE* HOME

Adding a dark wooden headboard in the master bedroom brings a focal point to the room and strikes a bold note in the light, airy space. Although many of the materials in the house are reclaimed, the headboard was sourced from the high street. Rattan pendants suspended either side of the bed over simple wooden bedside tables bring soft, warm light to the room, making it a *hygge* space for the couple to retreat to at the end of their busy days working in product design and marketing.

SENSORY SPACE

The couple's compact bathroom overlooks the garden and is a calm, sensory space with light blush plaster walls and marble-effect porcelain tiles. The pale pink shower curtain creates a feminine contrast to the stone, and the ceiling-fixed curtain pole is a clever solution to the lack of a facing wall.

COASTAL COTTAGE

Living by the sea is a dream many of us secretly hold. Breathing in coastal air, watching the waves and listening to the sound of the ocean creates a sense of calm and wellbeing. The stresses of daily life instantly slipped away when we arrived at Island Cottage, which sits in a nature reserve surrounded by water close to Pagham Harbour on the south coast of the UK.

Dating back to the 1800s, this brick and flint cottage when first built would have been small, just a room deep, with an outhouse. However, over the years it had suffered numerous unsympathetic extensions/additions. When Athena and Mark bought it in 2015, the interior lacked light and was damp and draughty. It was a mishmash of different styles and materials and seemed to have lost its identity.

Luckily the couple, who grew up in the area and wanted to relocate back from London, were able to look past the jumbled layout (which led to the house being nicknamed Narnia by friends) and see the cottage's underlying potential. They worked closely with Paul Cashin Architects to unpick the work that had been done and to realize their vision of blending the house into the surrounding nature reserve.

Athena and Mark wanted to complement the local landscape by using natural materials for the exterior at the rear, replacing the existing white render with larch cladding. Planning was a challenge – resistance to the cladding took them by surprise given the existing materials, which were at odds with the surroundings. However, the couple didn't give up. They walked around the area taking photos of agricultural buildings to prove that vertical cladding would be in keeping with the location, and eventually they were given the go-ahead.

The architects were asked to devise a layout that would link the interior to the landscape and create a better sense of continuity. As you walk through the house, it is clear that they delivered on the brief. An extension/addition was built, to rationalize the space rather than to add to the house's footprint. Great attention was paid to the materials used for the walls and floors, which include lime plaster and timber to bring together the old and new parts of the house.

The heart of the home is the kitchen and dining area, which houses a modern black wood kitchen. Athena's brother owns a kitchen company and Mark's son is a CAD designer, so they had expert help to come up with a layout that would make the best use of the space. Oak panelling was added to the walls to contribute texture and warmth. Sliding glass oak-framed doors run across the back of the house where the dining table

ROUGH AND READY

Wall treatments throughout the house have been carefully considered (previous spread and above). Plastered and limewashed walls are juxtaposed with tactile wooden cladding, as in this cozy snug leading off the open-plan kitchen/diner and accessed through a reclaimed wooden sliding barn-style door. The vintage leather armchair teamed with a sheepskin has been carefully positioned to invite us in.

ISLAND LIVING

In the kitchen, a practical oversized island unit takes centre stage and provides ample storage (opposite). There is no seating area on the island as the couple prefer to eat at the dining table, from where they can enjoy the glorious views. The black cabinetry grounds the neutral colour scheme in this space and is softened by the wood-clad backdrop, which exudes warmth.

is situated and opens onto a cantilevered steel frame. The table was built by Athena's father from wide chestnut planks from a local woodyard. It can seat up to 12 people and is perfect for family meals and gatherings.

There are three bedrooms on the first floor, all unique in style and with a different view. Each one has fitted wardrobes/closets that offer practical storage, pale wooden floors and large rugs for a comfortable feel. The bathrooms continue the pared-back scheme, giving the house a calm Scandi feel.

The main sitting room is upstairs and makes the most of the views over the nature reserve. Plump sofas, Berber rugs, wide-plank oak flooring and a wood-burning stove create a cozy mood, while the oversized windows, roof light and patio door allow light to flood in. The decor here is neutral and relaxed. Mark and Athena also installed a wood burner in the downstairs snug to mimic the number of stoves and open fires the home would have had in the 'olden days' and to create an inviting atmosphere.

When it came to the furnishings, the couple wanted a home that exuded a feeling of relaxation and ease. They achieved this by sourcing items from salvage yards and second-hand stores that are full of charm and history and reference the seaside.

A collaborative approach between a group of like-minded people, from architects to family members, along with Athena and Mark's creativity and connection to childhood memories, has enabled them to breathe new life into this historical cottage, transforming it into a contemporary Scandi Rustic haven.

NATURAL VIBES
At one end of the kitchen, the couple fitted a shelf made from waney/natural live-edged wood to display their collections of found objects and basketware (opposite). Statement oversized wicker lighting contributes further texture and a relaxed mood. That feeling is continued into the snug area, which is home to a tiled hearth and a freestanding wood-burning stove (above).

ROOM WITH A VIEW

As part of the renovation, Paul and Athena created an upstairs living room where they can enjoy uninterrupted views over the marshes beyond the garden (right). The decor here has an informal and relaxed Scandi feel. A brick wall has been left exposed to merge the old parts of the house with the new – as well as being aesthetically pleasing, it anchors the muted palette of off-whites and pale greys (above). The angular shape of the wood-burner's flue adds further architectural interest to the room.

UNDER THE COVERS

Statement lighting is a Scandi Rustic feature that this house has in abundance. In the main bedroom, an unusual pendant shade complements the softly textured limewashed plaster walls (this page). The same principle is applied in the guest bedroom, where a concrete pendant hangs low against pale grey panelling (opposite above left). Contrasting textures have been chosen for the soft furnishings and bedding to create an atmosphere that is restful but not bland.

HOME SPA VIBES

A restricted use of materials and pared-back design makes for a bathroom that feels like a spa-style sanctuary (opposite). The wooden-clad wall is an element that's repeated throughout the house and the oval-shaped bathtub enjoys centre stage. There is minimal fuss here, but the faux bark lampshades add a pleasing decorative detail.

RECLAIMED RUSTIC

Interior designer and stylist Kay Prestney grew up in a handsome Georgian home in the West Country before moving to London. It was there that she met husband Andy and bought a Victorian schoolhouse full of period charm.

After several fun-filled years in the capital, the couple started house hunting on the Suffolk/Essex borders in search of more space and a rural existence. Given Kay's love of quirky old homes, the last thing she thought they would buy was a 1980s house with no period features whatsoever.

However, with the birth of their first child imminent, the house, located in a small village close to where Andy grew up, offered them plenty of space and a blank canvas with which to work. It also came with a generous garden that had been lovingly maintained by the previous owners.

The premature arrival of daughter Bella temporarily brought renovation plans to a halt, but once they had settled into life as a family of three, Kay and Andy set to work transforming the house into a Scandi-inspired family home with lots of rustic charm.

When it came to the interior, Kay embraced the Japanese concept of wabi-sabi, which roughly translates as finding beauty in imperfection. However, this did not extend to embracing the swirled Artex textured plaster ceilings that they inherited. These were replastered and the flooring throughout the house was replaced. Wide-planked Scandinavian-style wood with a white oil finish was chosen for the sitting room, the upstairs landing and the loft, in order to create continuity between the spaces.

When it came to the couple's bedroom, a conversation with a friend led to the discovery of some beautiful wooden parquet flooring from an old naval vessel gathering dust in a garage. Restored to its former glory. it adds warmth and texture to the cozy room, which looks out over an old walnut tree.

One by one, the 1980s internal doors throughout the house were replaced with reclaimed ones found on Kay's 'vintiquing' trips. None of the doors are the same, but this is part of the charm - everything in this home has its own story to tell. When we stepped through the stable-style front door into the hallway with its brick-laid floor, it was almost impossible to imagine that the house was only built 30 years ago.

The couple added another storey, which serves as an office, additional living space and occasional bedroom. With double-height ceilings, a monochrome-inspired interior and a mezzanine level, it feels like a cool loft apartment in Copenhagen.

Downstairs, large glass sliding doors stretching the width of the living room open the house up to the outdoors. During the

summer, the family spend lots of time in the garden, which they have adapted to include a barbecue and eating area, a petanque court and raised vegetable beds. The most recent addition is a garden room that Kay built using mostly reclaimed and salvaged materials. Nestled in a corner of the garden, it is a beautiful and inspiring retreat.

In winter, the family make the most of the spacious living room, cuddling up on a large corner sofa layered with cushions, sheepskins and blankets. To inject character into this space, a brickwork chimneybreast and wood-burning stove were added. The clean modern lines of the wood burner (an ex-display bargain found by Andy) create a contemporary contrast to the rustic bricks. Kay's upcycling skills have been used to create a reading area out of packing crates and a wooden countertop salvaged from a florist. A wicker pendant light discovered in an antiques shop in Belgium pools soft light into this corner.

Inventive vintage solutions, including a repurposed railway station sorting rack, are used to store Andy's collection of vinyl. His decks live on top of an old sideboard that's placed on castors so that it can be pulled out when friends come over to party with a few bottles of wine and their favourite records.

With love, patience and a focus on sustainability, Kay and Andy have proven that you don't need a huge budget to create a warm and welcoming home that enhances a sense of wellbeing. Clever use of materials and treasured vintage finds have given this 1980s diamond in the rough a sense of history and rustic charm.

SOCIABLE SPACES

The house enjoys a large split-level living/dining space that allows this sociable family to host frequent dinner parties and gatherings. As part of Kay's job as an interior stylist, she often shoots features for magazines offering inspiring ideas for tablescapes that have been set up on this dining table. The seating around the table is an eclectic mix of vintage finds picked up over the years. Homemade linen bunting criss-crosses the ceiling, adding to the rustic feel.

GENTLE TEXTURES
The kitchen is a room that has evolved slowly over time with incremental rather than drastic changes. The most recent updates include the creation of an archway between the kitchen and dining room and plastering the kitchen walls in raw plaster sealed with varnish. This brings a soft, natural feel to the space and creates the perfect backdrop for Kay's collection of handmade ceramics.

LOVE IS HERE!

SPACE TO BREATHE

One of the biggest changes the couple made to the house was to add another floor above the living room. The new space functions as an additional reception room/office and spare bedroom. It has a dramatic double-height ceiling and a mezzanine level that's reached via a ladder.

All is pretty.

Andy Warhol

Moderna Museet,
Stockholm Sweden
10/2–17/3 1968

SIMPLE SLEEP SPACES

Upstairs the bedrooms lead off a corridor lined with family photos displayed in a mix of different frames. The couple's bedroom, with a parquet floor salvaged from an old naval ship, looks out onto a large walnut tree and feels like it is nestled in the treetops (opposite). In daughter Bella's room Kay has cleverly made a small room feel larger by using a reclaimed sliding door (above).

BATHING BEAUTIES

The house has two bathrooms. The family bathroom is on the first floor and features a rolltop tub and quirky lighting made from old lobster nets (above left). Downstairs there's a shower room with glazed zellige tiles and a basin resting on an old whitewashed cupboard (left). In this room, Kay has created a parquet-style wooden wall from old pallets.

RECLAIMED RETREAT

Kay's passion for sustainability can be seen in the inventive way in which she has used reclaimed materials wherever possible. Nowhere is this ingenuity more in evidence than in the garden room that she has recently created using almost entirely salvaged materials and other finds (above). The idea for the project was sparked by the discovery of some beautiful old windows on one of her 'vintiquing' trips and the wood-clad cabin now provides a wonderful oasis from everyday life in a corner of the garden (opposite).

SCANDI ELEGANCE

Many of us idly dream of owning our own shop, but few succeed in making that dream become a reality. For Lisa Brass, owner of Scandinavian lifestyle brand Design Vintage, the chance discovery of a small shop space behind her Brighton home was the catalyst for a new career as a shopkeeper.

Lisa was working as an interior designer at the time and had been looking for a studio for her design work, but after taking on the space she began to sell a selection of vintage homeware. It was to prove so popular that Lisa decided to relocate back to the Chichester area where she grew up in order to give Design Vintage, her burgeoning business, a new, much larger, home.

Having found a converted barn overlooking a lake that would make the perfect shop premises, Lisa and husband Stuart started the search for a family home close by. As luck would have it, they soon stumbled across a detached Georgian house dating back to 1804 and in need of complete renovation in the village where Lisa grew up.

Untouched for over 25 years, with maroon floors, yellow walls and a pervading smell of damp, the house screamed money pit. However, its location, just ten minutes from West Wittering beach, persuaded the couple to take it on. Walking into the hallway of the house for the first time, it was easy to see why they decided to take the plunge.

The house feels wonderfully open and spacious, with floor-to-ceiling sash windows that allow light to pour into the handsome and well-proportioned Georgian rooms. While the architecture dates back to the 1800s, Lisa has brought the interior up to date with a Scandi-inspired makeover.

Floors have been painstakingly stripped back to reveal their beautiful natural tones and given a white oil finish throughout the house. The ground floor was opened up by knocking down the wall between the living room and kitchen and installing original Crittall metal-framed doors in the divide. The doors were sourced from eBay and carefully restored by Stuart, who originally trained as a carpenter. Unfortunately, the original sash windows could not be rescued but they were removed and closely copied by a local joinery firm. Fitted with a slimline double-glazing system and painted a crisp black, they retain the original character of the house and fit seamlessly into the monochrome interior.

In the living room, taking down the ceilings then whitewashing and exposing the beams has created a wonderful sense of space. The addition of a wood-burning stove, rattan statement lighting and an oversized wooden coffee table to display treasured items brings a sense of warmth and coziness.

LIGHT AND BRIGHT

Installing original Crittall doors found on eBay between the kitchen and living room has opened up Lisa's house and helped to draw light into the darker rear portion. In the living room, large white linen sofas are gathered around a coffee table inviting you to take a seat and relax. Throughout the house, wooden floors with a white oil finish create a sense of calm – it's hard to imagine that they were once painted a dark maroon colour.

OPEN HOUSE

Adding a wood-burning stove to the living space means that despite the high ceilings and large windows the room still feels cozy in winter (above). One of our favourite features in this room is the oversized olive tree that sits in the corner in a large earthenware pot. A vintage wooden table occupies the heart of the kitchen with stools around it creating an informal feel (opposite). Locker-style cupboards painted white house Lisa's cookery books, while pasta, rice and cereals are stored in Kilner-style jars.

The choice of white walls throughout the house (apart from in the utility room off the kitchen) creates a calm backdrop for a clever blend of Scandinavian and vintage furnishings. It is this mix of modern and rustic that has become the Design Vintage hallmark. Lisa scours the globe to source both period and contemporary pieces for her home and shop. One of her most precious finds is a feathered crown from Swedish brand Love Warriors that hangs on the sitting room wall close to the deep linen sofas, adding a delicate texture to the room.

Upstairs, the renovation work included removing an awkwardly positioned shower room then, perhaps controversially for some, sacrificing a bedroom to add a spacious second bathroom. This 'girls bathroom', with its freestanding tub, patterned encaustic tiles and large picture window, is Lisa's favourite room. The outdoors is brought in to create a spa feel, with a large olive tree in the corner echoing the softly swaying trees in the garden beyond. Although the room has a decadent feel, the rolltop bathtub was an eBay bargain that Lisa painted and restored with a new set of taps/faucets. The mirror, medicine cabinet and rustic bench are all vintage finds.

The renovation is an ongoing process. Last year, the couple knocked through into the loft to create a luxurious master suite with lime-plastered walls. In the longer term, they plan to remove the unsympathetic uPVC conservatory that's tacked onto the back of the kitchen and to build a contemporary black-clad Scandinavian-style extension/addition in its place.

MONOCHROME STYLE
Black Shaker-style cabinets with brass handles on one side of the kitchen contrast with contemporary white units on the other (opposite). Crittall metal-framed doors lead to a utility/boot room. Narrow marble worksurfaces are used on both sides of the room for a sense of continuity (above).

However, Design Vintage is going from strength to strength, with successful London pop-ups and a second store in Guildford, so it may take a little time for those plans to become reality. In the meantime, the family can enjoy the changing seasons on West Wittering beach before returning home to the small slice of Scandinavia they have created in West Sussex.

RESTFUL SPACES

While some people hide their household linens away from view, Lisa has used a vintage armoire to make a decorative feature of her collection. Fitting wall mounted lights either side of the bed frees up space in this compact bedroom. In the bathroom, a coat of dark paint and the addition of new taps/faucets has breathed fresh life into an old rolltop bathtub (opposite).

HOME IN THE WOODS

Nestled in a pocket of ancient woodland in the most western part of Cornwall lies a hidden house surrounded by six acres of trees and pasture, a small stream and an abundance of wildlife.

A pipe dream turned into reality when designers and makers Tom and Danielle Raffield relocated from their seaside home on the Cornish coast to a woodland setting where they could make the outdoors and living with nature their priority. The couple use wood to handcraft lighting and pieces of furniture that resemble forms found in nature, so this was the perfect backdrop to inspire their work.

The plot they found allowed them the space for a workshop as well as a home for their growing brood (they now have three children). They also inherited a number of existing outbuildings dotted around the plot, including a small 19th-century Grade II-listed building made from granite, cob and Delabole slate, which would originally have been a gamekeeper's cottage and is known locally as the Gingerbread House.

The couple designed and built a timber-and-steel framed house that seamlessly connects to the old cottage and is known as the steam-bent house. When planning the new house, their goal was to create a structure that would blend with the natural world and blur the lines between outdoors and indoors by using materials offered up by the surroundings. To achieve this, ash was used for the exterior and the interior was

finished with fallen trees from their own land. We were struck by the way in which the curved design softens the building's impact and melds it into the landscape.

The build was not straightforward. It involved many parties and a lengthy planning process, which took two years. To keep costs down, the couple moved into the gamekeeper's cottage, which at the time had no running hot water or heating, no bathroom or kitchen and a mud floor. Although the living conditions were less than ideal (especially with a three-month-old baby) the couple's determination to create their dream home along with the magic of the woodland setting kept them going.

The interior design is very much an extension of the surrounding landscape, with the focus placed on drawing nature inside. Every space within the house has doors opening onto the woods and the goal was to embrace and complement the backdrop using natural materials and textures wherever possible. Perhaps surprisingly for homeware designers, Tom and Dani care very little for wallpapers, curtains and ornaments. Their most treasured possessions are handmade, gifted or inherited, and they value emotional connections over current trends.

HEART OF THE HOME

The kitchen is at the centre of the open-plan living space. It ticks every Scandi Rustic box, from the layering of texture and use of natural materials to Tom's bold statement lighting.

At the centre of the house is an open-plan kitchen and dining room. This is where the old cottage and new house merge, and it is spacious and comfortable. There is a wood-lined passage to the old cottage made of Cornish larchwood and glass. The cottage is used as an informal cozy family living area with a wood-burning stove, a comfy sofa and an abundance of books.

There are five bedrooms in total, with each of the children having a room of their own. They are all slightly different yet unified by the principle of embracing natural materials. Even the main family bathroom is clad entirely in wood, which brings an amazing warmth both in terms of heat retention and aesthetic. It has the feel of a Nordic sauna and the wood has proved surprisingly practical and durable, with no sign of water stains despite frequent splashing at bathtime.

We couldn't talk about this house without mentioning the dramatic staircase. The curved design is made up of 120 steam-bent strips of sustainable ash, oak and walnut that blend together casting beautiful shapes and shadows. The curves draw your eye to a double-height space that showcases Tom's Giant Flock Chandelier, a beautiful statement light that's fast becoming an iconic design. The couple say they love seeing people's reactions the first time they look up and see it. More like an art installation than a light fitting, it certainly commanded our attention.

This house has been a true labour of love, with the couple literally using their own hands to craft it layer by layer. The result is

TONES AND TEXTURES
Natural textures such as the jute rugs, boho-style cushions and floaty linen curtains complement the neutral colour palette, wooden backdrop and steam-bent furniture, which makes the sociable living space and thoroughfare to the master bedroom snug and inviting.

a home that feels uniquely creative and nurturing. Tom and Dani's focus on materials and texture means not a single wall, floor or ceiling has been forgotten. Every inch of this house is engaging and has a story to tell. It would not look out of place in a Swedish forest as it echoes the design of Scandinavian cabins in using natural honest materials and celebrating simplicity in design.

DREAMY BEDROOMS

A cluster of steam-bent wooden light fittings made by Tom make a dramatic statement in the master bedroom (opposite). There are personal details here too, with shelves and a gallery wall displaying special mementoes. The children's rooms have been given the same attention to detail as the rest of the house (this page). Whitewashed wooden cladding offers a calming backdrop and there are even pieces of steam-bent furniture to house favourite toys (above right).

SAUNA STYLE

The mixed-wood cladding continues into the family bathroom, which was inspired by a traditional wooden Swedish sauna or *bastu* (opposite). Tom and Dani wanted to make the bathroom both functional and relaxing, and although it's a relatively small space there has been no compromise on style. One of Tom's handcrafted lights, the Urchin Pendant, creates patterns of shadow when dimmed and is the perfect ambient lighting for a bathroom.

INTERESTING CONTRASTS

The beech, ash, Norwegian spruce and sweet chestnut planks that line the bathroom all came from Tom and Dani's woodland and bring many benefits – they are beautiful, durable and retain heat well (above right). In the bathroom the natural tones and grain of the wood contrasts with the right angles of a concrete basin, which brings a more masculine edge to the room (above left).

RUSTIC BOLTHOLE

In a sleepy rural hamlet a few miles inland from the wide expanses of Perranporth beach is a very special holiday hideaway. Tucked away at the end of a winding Cornish country lane lies The Hide.

The first time Sarah Stanley visited the site in the spring of 2015, she knew she had found the ultimate sanctuary from busy city life. Although the plot was carved out of the garden of a traditional thatched cottage, from the outset Sarah wanted to create something more contemporary.

The brief to architects Studio Arc was to base the design around the idea of a bird hide, using a palette of wood, concrete and glass to seamlessly blend the building into the landscape. Wooden shingle cladding was chosen for much of the exterior as it ages to a shimmering silvery grey hue that echoes the surrounding woodland.

Approaching the house up a steep track, it is hard to believe that there was once a crumbling carport where The Hide now stands. Pushing open the sturdy wooden gate, one of the first things you notice is the overhanging glass windows that project from the bedroom and living area. Although they caused some headaches during the build, these have proved to be one of the most successful parts of the design, allowing you to feel part of nature while cocooned inside.

The house is designed as a retreat for two, comprising an open-plan living-dining area, kitchen, bathroom, bedroom and outside terrace, all on one level. In the summer the terrace serves as an extension of the interior, with the garden beyond containing a hot tub, barbecue and firepit. Mats and blocks are also provided, allowing visitors to start their day with yoga on the terrace.

It is this level of attention to detail that has allowed Sarah to build up her successful travel business Unique Homestays. The company offers a hand-picked selection of luxury self-catering accommodation (including The Hide) that combines inspiring locations with thought-provoking design.

The interior of the Hide certainly delivers on the thought-provoking design. Echoing the exterior, the same limited selection of materials has been used to great effect inside. The walls and floors are pale grey concrete and reclaimed wood has been used for the kitchen cabinets, wardrobes and doors to add texture. In the bedroom and living space, statement rattan pendant lights create a dramatic focal point.

However, it was the deep window seats created by the overhanging window that runs the length of the living space that stole our hearts. Dressed with cozy sheepskins and piles of natural linen cushions, this is the perfect place to curl up and watch the rain falling in the colder months. At night, you can gaze up at the

RAW APPEAL
The Hide is a bolthole made for two. The living and sleeping spaces are divided by a door made from reclaimed floorboards affixed to a sliding rail. When this door is open the interior feels like one large continuous space, thanks to the use of a consistent palette of materials

BACK TO NATURE

The design for the house was based around the concept of a bird hide, with cedar shingle cladding used on much of the exterior so it harmonizes with the surrounding landscape (above). One of the most unique design features are the large projecting windows, which create deep window seats in the living space and allow you to gaze up at the stars while lying in bed (opposite).

stars that fill the wide-open skies over the Cornish countryside beyond.

Adding to the sense of *hygge* is an open fire in the corner of the living space with logs stacked underneath. A deep green velvet sofa in the centre of the space invites you to take a seat. Choosing a rich, verdant green for the sofa upholstery is another clever way of echoing the natural world that surrounds The Hide. And although the house is used as a holiday let, displays of vintage finds including wood blocks, books and old jugs create a sense of home.

In another corner of the living space, peephole windows have been added to the wall to create a dappled light effect that's reminiscent of sunlight falling gently through trees. The same windows appear in the bathroom, which features an oversized concrete bathtub that was originally created for use as an animal trough and took five men to lift into place during the build. The waffled linen robes provided for visitors add a spa-like feeling to this room.

Underfloor heating throughout the house means the concrete floors are always warm and smooth underfoot. After a day out spent exploring the rugged beaches and hidden coves of the Cornish coast, a deeply comfortable bed layered with linen bedding, cushions and throws beckons you to snuggle down under the softest of duvets.

Thanks to innovative design, careful use of materials and a focus on creating a house that is both inspired by and embedded in the surrounding landscape, the Stanleys have created a truly relaxing rustic haven.

SLEEPING QUARTERS

Concrete is one of the main materials used for both interior and exterior finishes. In the bedroom both the walls and floors have a smooth pale grey concrete finish while reclaimed wooden doors and wardrobes provide contrast and add warmth (opposite and above). Underfloor heating adds *hygge*, as does bed linen in soft natural fibres and piles of soft cushions on the bed.

UNCLUTTERED LUXE

In the bathroom, the main talking point is a huge concrete bath that was once an old animal trough (this page). Tiny cut-outs echo the concept of a bird hide, allowing shards of light to enter and creating nooks for display (left and above left).

CABIN LIFE

The story of how Elin and Jonas came to live in Vendelsö, a family-friendly neighbourhood with lots of green space located just south of Stockholm, Sweden, is a familiar one. Ten years ago, they were a young professional couple renting a flat in Stockholm when their first baby came along.

Short on space, and with Stockholm one of the most expensive places to buy property in Europe, the couple decided to move out of the city in order to realize the dream of owning their own home. Jonas grew up close to Vendelsö, so the move also meant that the couple would be closer to family.

As we drove out of Stockholm, passing forests, fields and lakes on the way to the couple's house, it was easy to understand why they wanted to put down roots in this area. We finally arrived at a cluster of traditional Swedish wooden cabins, most of them painted black with white window frames, low apex roofs and outdoor porches covered in festoon lights.

The 130sq m/1399 sq ft cabin that Jonas and Elin bought was constructed in 1969. Over the last decade, they have made lots of improvements, fitting in the DIY around their growing family. The couple have deliberately taken their time with the renovation of their home, living in the space and getting to know it before making any decisions that they might later regret.

Elin is an interior stylist and had a clear vision of how she wanted the cabin to look and feel, so she took the lead when it came to designing the interior while Jonas was charged with using his DIY skills to implement Elin's ideas. They tore down walls to optimize the cabin's footprint and removed the internal doors (apart from the bedrooms and bathroom) to create the illusion of more space and to improve the flow from one room to the next.

The couple also changed the existing kitchen layout to accommodate a central island unit, which is a great use of space. We particularly enjoyed the way the modern smoked oak kitchen cabinets contrast with the soft white walls, grey-beige countertops and chunky wooden accessories.

Open-plan living is as popular in Sweden as elsewhere, but Elin and Jonas have ensured their open-plan kitchen/living area feels cozy by placing a wood-burning stove at the heart of the space. The couple have also created a *hygge* corner in the kitchen by building a deep ledge below a large window to create a reading nook that overlooks the garden. There's storage underneath for logs, which injects a rustic feel. With the addition of texture in the form of cushions and a sheepskin, it's a snug spot that you feel the urge to grab a blanket and retreat to.

DARK AND HANDSOME

Elin and Jonas have created a cosy, open-plan
living space by applying key design principles.
A clever lighting scheme, use of different
textures and a traditional wood-burning stove
bring warmth and character to the home.

In the main living areas, the colour palette is neutral and calming, while the bedrooms have a romantic, feminine feel, with touches of pink and soft linens. Their daughters' bedrooms are particularly magical, with areas for relaxing, crafting and playing.

After a decade in their home the couple are still not finished with their renovation plans. Next on the list is adding a second storey and decorating the family bathroom. What Elin and Jonas have achieved on a limited budget while raising a young family is inspiring. It demonstrates how creativity, clever choices, and unusual accessories can completely transform a blank canvas. It also proves that you don't need to have interesting architectural features to achieve your Scandi Rustic home of dreams.

IN THE PINK

A feminine colour palette flows throughout the private areas of this home, perhaps reflective of the tastes of interior designer Elin and her two young daughters. The master bedroom is soft and romantic in mood, with pretty finishing touches bringing the room to life (opposite). A simple wooden peg rail is the perfect place to display favourite items of clothing (above). And a desire to bring the outdoors in is evident from the dried flowers hanging from the rail and the delicate handmade wreath above the bed.

ROUGH LUXE

The bathroom is one of the few spaces where the gentle pastel palette is not evident (above). Instead, it echoes the tones of the black wood kitchen cabinets. This room has more of a masculine edge, thanks to the introduction of harder materials such as the dark grey concrete basin and glossy tiles. The sink is teamed with white marble tiles, which have been laid to show off their scalloped edges, and a brass tap/faucet. Limewash has been used to create the effect of raw concrete on the walls and an oversized vintage circular mirror hangs above the basin.

SOFTLY SOFTLY

The couple have created charming bedrooms for their two young daughters (this page and opposite), with whitewashed wooden floors and light walls to keep the space feeling fresh and bright. There is an abundance of quirky toys here, while the desk area offers a place to imagine, craft and create. A vintage armoire offers practical storages space and has been painted a cheerful yellow tone that brings a sense of playfulness and happiness to the room. Wicker baskets rather than plastic tubs are used to accommodate toys.

RUSTIC ROMANTIC

As we begin families of our own, the urge to return to the place where we grew up and formed cherished childhood memories becomes strong for many of us. For Anna and Johan, that place is Norrtälje, a small town buried deep in the Swedish countryside, surrounded by forests.

Leaving Stockholm behind, the couple found what can only be described as an idyllic spot in a rural location with plenty of land for their two young daughters and assorted animals, including rabbits, cats, a dog and ponies. The house itself is a typical red and white wooden Swedish farmhouse dating back to 1790 and is utterly charming. The couple don't know much about its history other than it was once a working farm. Indeed, its agricultural past is still evident from the space that surrounds the property, including the large garden, a greenhouse, stables and other outbuildings. During the summer the family spend lots of time outdoors, tending the garden, feeding the ponies and allowing the girls to roam free.

The farmhouse was structurally in good condition when the couple moved in, but it was in need of updating. They decided to focus on decorating rather than carrying out expensive building works, although the downstairs bathroom and kitchen were crying out for an overhaul. The couple had a clear vision for their new home – Anna is an interior designer and blogger while Johan, in Anna's words, is 'a great handyman and DIYer'. It's a match made in renovation heaven.

On arrival at the house, we stepped into a wonderfully romantic Swedish interior. A large glass porch leads into a hallway painted in warm neutral shades, and as we ventured through the ground floor, we realized that Anna and Johan have retained every scrap of the farmhouse's rustic charm. The couple decided against building a modern open-plan extension/addition and instead have focused on retaining each room's original purpose and distinct style.

The kitchen is where the family spend the majority of their time, cooking and entertaining family and friends. Anna chose to reflect the history of the house by sourcing a large vintage wooden table and chairs for the dining area. The kitchen units were painted in a soft, sludgy green shade, a colour that reappears throughout the house in different forms, from painted furniture to wallpaper to greenery.

In the living room, with its low, beamed ceilings, a wall of open shelving is painted in the same soft green and displays accessories, books and family photographs. Although Scandinavian design is often described as minimal, Anna is not afraid to use pattern to add texture and coziness to her home.

In the living room (and elsewhere in the house), Anna has chosen to use wallpaper designs that echo the natural landscape outside. This room leads onto a sunroom flooded with daylight from the large windows. There is an abundance of houseplants, a comfortable low-slung rattan sofa and an antique dresser adorned with beautiful ceramics and vintage kitchenalia.

The upper floor is reached via a winding wooden staircase. Here, the tranquil and understated master bedroom boasts a calming tonal palette. Anna opted for mineral paint throughout the house – a popular finish with Danes and Swedes. It's a traditional limewash paint that possesses a matte chalky texture and depth of colour that brings the walls to life and

only improves with age. The children's bedrooms are perfectly in harmony with the rest of the house, with antique armoires, plenty of rattan storage and adorable Mrs Mighetto wallpaper.

Anna and Johan's home is full of vintage finds, warm earthy tones and seasonal touches. And while you may look at these pictures and conclude that it is finished, in fact the couple still have DIY plans at the forefront of their minds, including making space for a family bathroom upstairs.

Anna and Johan have managed to retain the atmosphere of this traditional farmhouse while creating a warm, cozy and modern family home for modern times. The house exudes individuality and personality and was a joy to experience.

LIGHT AND BRIGHT
The sunroom is a Scandi Rustic triumph. The muted colour palette and touches of green in the form of plants and painted furniture set a timeless, serene mood. Antique furniture adds rustic charm to this space, where the family gather for home-cooked meals beneath the statement handmade linen lampshade. This well-lit room is also the perfect place to grow seedlings and propagate plants.

CALM AND COLLECTED
A view through into the kitchen/dining room
shows how the sage green accent colour and
limewashed walls make this functional, busy
area feel calm and relaxed (opposite). The tactile
marble countertops, vintage kitchenalia, touches
of brass and copper and terracotta pots bring a
warm, earthy aesthetic to the space (this page).

BOTANICAL CHARM

The couple have made the large living room homey and inviting by adding patterned wallpaper and an oversized modern coffee table (opposite). There are plants strategically placed along the windowsill behind the linen sofa, which make for an interesting backdrop, and a playful monochrome gallery wall plus a cluster of artworks propped against the wall for a relaxed vibe.

ADDING INTEREST

Floor-to-ceiling cabinetry and open shelving is painted in the muted sage green shade that recurs throughout the house and provides valuable storage space, with the bottom section offering closed cupboards to conceal everyday clutter (above). Anna has used the open shelves to create artful vignettes made up of glass and ceramic pieces, family photos and interior design books.

A PLACE FOR DREAMING

The master bedroom on the first floor is pared back in style with a simple tone-on-tone colour palette based around the soft earthy shade that covers the walls (opposite). The bed is layered with linens for an elegant and serene scene.

FAMILY FOCUSED

A whimsical woodland atmosphere has been created in the couple's daughters' bedrooms, with a swan rug and wallpapered walls (above left and right). A vintage glazed armoire houses dusty pink and beige linens and stacking boxes for keepsakes. The bathroom is traditional in design (right).

HOME BY THE SEA

After a decade of city living in Copenhagen and Paris, in 2014 Pernille Grønkjær Taatø returned to Hornbaek, the small coastal Danish town where she grew up, to put down new roots close to the sea with her husband and three children.

The chance discovery of a building plot just three doors away from Pernille's childhood home set the couple on the path to designing and building their dream family home. The house is nestled on the outskirts of Hornbaek, a quiet little town about 45 minutes north of Copenhagen. Sleepy in the winter, it comes to life during the summer months when city dwellers decamp to their summer houses, drawn by the long white sandy beaches backed by pine forests.

It was the wooden construction, simple black exteriors and white windows of those classic Danish summer houses that informed the design of the home the couple decided to build. They drew up the plans themselves and it was important to them that the house fitted in with the local landscape and architecture. As a result, it looks as though it has always had a place on the street.

The dark, unassuming exterior conceals a wonderfully light, bright interior. Although white interiors can feel clinical, this certainly isn't the case in Pernille's home. A limited palette of materials and colours has been used throughout the house to create a sense of calm tranquillity. White walls, pale wooden floors and timber-clad ceilings create a soothing backdrop for artworks painted by Pernille, vintage objects collected on the family's travels and foliage and driftwood foraged from the coast.

The house is a simple L-shape with four bedrooms and two bathrooms and a spacious open-plan living space with vaulted ceilings. This makes up the kitchen, dining and living area and is where the family congregates for breakfast around the kitchen island and to watch television from the large comfortable corner sofa. The hero of this open-plan area has to be the monumental 3.5 metre/12ft rustic wooden dining table, which plays host to dinner parties with friends and family who take a seat on Hans Wegner's Wishbone chairs, a Scandinavian design classic. There are further nods to modern Danish design in the living area, where a Poul Kjaerholm PK22 wicker chair creates a cozy spot to relax with a coffee and stack of magazines.

Everything about this home has been kept simple and pared back, with just a few carefully chosen stand-out pieces and materials elevating the space. For example, while the kitchen units are from Ikea, the couple invested in a Douglas fir countertop from Dinesen for the long island unit, which adds a wonderful sense of warmth and texture to the space. Artisan-crafted leather

handles replace the standard Ikea ones on the kitchen cabinets as well as on the Pax wardrobes in the bedroom to lend a more expensive, luxurious feel to the interiors.

The bathrooms follow a simple design using the same materials; black slate floors that are warm underfoot, classic large white metro-style tiles and crisp, contemporary basins in white porcelain. Each bathroom is home to a vintage medicine cabinet, adding character to the space and avoiding any sense of clutter.

While the house has a relatively modest footprint (a deliberate choice), it never feels small or crowded on account of the double-height timber-clad ceilings that the couple made central to the design. We loved the sense of space that this helped to create. As the layout is arranged around the garden, nearly all of the rooms have external doors that connect the inside with the outdoors. Festoon lights strung around a covered outdoor terrace glimmer on the long Scandinavian summer evenings when the family eat dinner outside.

Just a short walk from the house lies Hornbaek's pretty little harbour, bobbing with brightly coloured fishing vessels and traditional wooden rowing boats. Long sunbleached pontoons lead out to black-clad bathing huts where locals come to take a sauna after a bracing swim in the sea. The family keep a small sailing boat here that they use to explore the scenic Danish coastline before returning home from long days on the water to the quiet calm of the beautiful home they have created.

MIXING HIGH AND LOW

Mixing affordable Ikea staples with more expensive Scandinavian design classics is a recipe for success in Pernille's home. Such items sit happily alongside each other in the spacious open-plan living space. Saving money by choosing a simple white corner sofa from Ikea meant that Pernille was able to invest in modern classics such as the PK22 chair (opposite above left) and the Bestlite by Best & Lloyd (opposite below right).

RAISE THE ROOF
The couple's decision to opt for a double-height ceiling means that the living space feels wonderfully spacious. Adding timber cladding to the ceilings is a clever design trick that adds character to the newly built house. The Hans Wegner chairs around the rustic dining table are another Danish design classic that add a timeless feel to the interior.

BOLD CONTRASTS

The dark cladding of the exterior of the house belies the light, bright Scandinavian interior that lies within (opposite and this page). While Pernille is a fan of contemporary design, she has also mixed vintage and reclaimed items into the interior, like the earthenware pot used to store utensils in the kitchen.

KEEP IT SIMPLE

Nothing in this home is fussy or overcomplicated. The success of the interior lies in allowing everything enough space to breathe. The white walls create a soothing backdrop and allow you to focus on carefully curated displays and beautiful items such as the intricate embroidered wallhanging in the bedroom (left). There are two bathrooms, both of which follow the same successful recipe of simple white wall tiles contrasting with dark slate floors (below).

ALL SERENE

The overwhelming sense when you step into Pernille's house is one of peace. This tranquillity is created, in part, by the clever use of storage to contain the inevitable chaos of everyday life. The corridor leading to the bedrooms has a long run of cabinets attached to the wall (opposite). To maximize the feeling of space. Dinesen Douglas fir flooring has been used throughout the house, creating a sense of consistency. The long, wide planks with a pale finish draw the eye down the corridor to the bathroom.

IN THE CITY

Amagerbro is where the sea meets the city in Copenhagen, and it is here that Susan Mogensen and her husband Daniel chose to take on an ambitious renovation project, turning a run-down commercial building into a cozy rustic family home.

While many people might have been daunted by taking on such a large project with young children in tow, renovation runs in the family for Susan, whose parents owned their own building company. Daniel is a professional plumber, and the couple had already renovated one apartment when they stumbled across a building in their favourite neighbourhood with the potential to offer them the extra space they needed for their growing family.

It took imagination to look beyond the stark white walls and shiny blue vinyl floors that greeted them and to see how this space could become a family home full of warmth and character. The building itself had a rich and varied history, having started life as a cigar factory in the early 1900s. It was owned at that time by an elderly gentlemen called Mr Bertlesen, who drowned after falling overboard when sailing to Belgium. It later gained notoriety as the first building from which porn was sold in Denmark, with travellers from all around the world flying into nearby Kastrup airport to pay it a visit.

By the time the couple came to view it, this latter use had fortunately ceased, but the building was in a poor state of repair and offered no living accommodation

whatsoever. Having secured the purchase of the property, the first task was a complete redesign of the layout. The interior was so big that it was possible to divide it into two separate apartments, with the top floor given over to Susan's sister and her partner. In the downstairs apartment, a large open-plan kitchen/diner was planned in the space where an office had previously been situated and what had once been a small kitchen where the office workers made their tea became the family bathroom.

Unphased by the scale of the challenge, the couple undertook all the construction work themselves, working late into the evenings and at weekends to transform the building. They only brought in external tradesmen to help build the orangery that leads off the kitchen.

Although they were working to a tight budget, the couple placed a strong emphasis on sustainability in all their design and construction choices. Reclaimed and recycled materials were used wherever possible, and these have been key to bringing interest and personality back into the house. Nowhere is this more evident than in the kitchen-diner, where Susan chose to lay a reclaimed brick floor in a herringbone

pattern. This proved to be something of a labour of love – it took six months just to cut the bricks before the couple could even start to lay the floor. However, it has helped to restore some of the original character of the building that was lost, bringing a much-needed layer of texture to the space.

Although modern units were used for the kitchen carcases, the fronts were made from old scaffold planks rescued from a local building company. Washing the planks down and treating them with organic rapeseed oil has instilled them with a rich rustic feel. The couple opted for open shelving rather than wall cabinets in order to create a more relaxed and informal feeling in the kitchen.

In a further piece of recycling, the wooden floor of the old office has been taken up and relaid in parquet style in the couple's bedroom. To create continuity, texture has also been carried through into the bathroom, where pebbles foraged from the local beach have been used to create the floor. A smooth concrete finish was applied to the walls, providing a neutral backdrop to a rugged wooden boat-style bathtub and a sink made from a salvaged tin trough. The brass taps/faucets and shower fittings were one of the few new items in the apartment that Susan splurged on, and they add a subtly luxurious touch to the bathroom.

We loved the way that Susan has blended together new and old and her use of vintage furniture throughout the apartment. From the dining table sourced at a favourite thrift store in Sweden to the old school lockers used to store toys in the girls' bedrooms, this is a home overflowing with stories and

HOME AGAIN
The apartment was converted back into residential use by the couple after a long period as a commercial building. The couple have used reclaimed materials wherever possible to restore character and warmth to the space. The kitchen units are made from old scaffold boards rubbed down with rapeseed oil to give them a rich wooden hue (opposite). Concrete worktops contrast with the wood and add an industrial edge.

character. There are still elements of the building yet to be finished, such as the entrance hall shared by the siblings, but Susan has already started to think about taking on another renovation project when this one is complete.

MORE IS MORE

Susan is a Scandi maximalist. Her rustic-inspired home blends textures, colours and objects to create a cozy, inviting feel. In the dining room, industrial-style shelving brims with vintage finds, books and plants.

IN THE PINK

Although many of the materials used in the apartment have an industrial quality, the decor still feels soft and inviting thanks to Susan's chosen colour palette. In the main bedroom the walls are painted in a blush pink, creating a soothing atmosphere (opposite). Against this backdrop sit linen bedding and cushions in natural colours with ombre tones used as an accent. A scaffold-board shelf above the bed displays a blend of contemporary and vintage homeware. There are hand-drawn prints, ceramic vases and displays of dried grasses such as pampas.

LIVING LIFE IN COLOUR

With lots of hard work and late nights devoted to carrying out much of the renovation work themselves, the couple have created a family home full of life and atmosphere. In the girls' bedrooms, Susan has embraced colour, choosing a rich teal blue for the walls with accessories such as the bed canopy in a contrasting mustard. A corner nook has been wallpapered in a sweet bug and butterfly wallpaper and is used as an open wardrobe to display the girl's clothes (above left).

SPA-STYLE SANCTUARY

While much of the renovation was done on a tight budget and using salvaged materials wherever possible, there were a few areas where Susan invested in more expensive items. The bathroom is one such area. Here Susan opted for brass taps/faucets and shower fittings to add a luxurious feel to the space. The wooden boat-style tub was another investment item (opposite). However, to balance out this spending the floor was laid from rocks and pebbles collected from the local beach and an old tin tub used for the vanity unit (right).

ARCHITECTURAL SIMPLICITY

Masahiro and Mette's summer house offers breathtaking views of the Danish coast. A successful fusion of Danish and Japanese design and cultures, it is sensitive to its surroundings and allows the landscape to take centre stage.

Architects Masahiro Katsume and Mette Fredskild have created their dream weekend house in a coastal town that's just an hour's drive from their home in Copenhagen. It's a relaxing haven far from the hustle and bustle of city life.

From the moment we set eyes on Masahiro and Mette's house, we knew how special it was. Every detail has been meticulously planned. It feels like the building, nestled among trees beside a lake, has been part of the landscape forever. However, it was actually built in 2019, replacing an old hut that stood on the plot when the couple first came to view the land. The site is known locally as the 'forest at the waterfront' because it is one of the few that has retained its trees, and it was this unique location with which the couple fell in love.

Mette is Danish and Masahiro is Japanese, and after 25 years together, this house has allowed them to realize their ideal way of living, fusing together their two cultures. The couple made a decision not to rush the design and construction process but instead to take a slow and considered approach. Instead of tearing down the original hut, they spent weekends in it for a year to give them a better feel for the

surroundings. Masahiro studied the way the light moved across the plot throughout the seasons, while Mette concentrated on the internal spaces and practical requirements. As with all new builds, there were planning laws and guidance to take into account, but luckily this was an area that the couple were well versed in. In 2018, construction began on their black-clad modular home, set slightly back from the coast to make the most of the spectacular views.

Upon approach, all that can be seen is a single cherry tree – the deliberately naturalistic garden is one of many carefully made decisions that make this home unique. A concrete deck raised above ground level leads to the entrance. The exterior is part-wooden, part-steel frame and expresses a fusion of typically Japanese and modern Scandinavian architectural styles.

The house has been built in separate sections to create a structure that is not too overbearing and avoids the strong seasonal winds that buffet the coast. It is positioned to capture the daylight and the huge glass windows frame views of the landscape. The couple were inspired by Japanese writer Junichiro Tanizaki's essay 'In Praise of Shadows', about the beauty of contrasts.

The entrance hall provides a view of the rear garden and the sea beyond. It's paved with smooth pebbles and functions as a connecting zone between the living and sleeping areas. Mette and Mashahiro wanted to include references to Japanese culture, and a basin situated in the entrance hall allows incomers to wash their hands upon entering. This multifunctional space also provides storage, a laundry area and bookshelves.

Moving into the open-plan interior, we were taken aback by the drama of the double-height room and the sense of light and space here. The ceiling and walls above the windows are clad in charred wood, which adds a tactile, rustic element and the space is zoned into areas designed for specific activities – yoga, painting and watching movies. Mette and Mashahiro have a son and daughter who visit frequently and the family enjoy the views and sense of remoteness in this area. The couple limited the height of the sliding windows to 2m/6½ feet because they wanted a home that was sympathetic to its surroundings rather than what they describe as 'sensationalist'.

The house is triumphantly minimalist. There are no decorative flourishes – instead, it contemplates and celebrates the natural landscape, the woodland and the sea. When it came to the interior, Mette drew inspiration from this landscape, decorating the living area with plants and foraged finds. It's rich in texture and objects with a story to tell.

Mette and Masahiro's home celebrates simplicity in design and the mantra of less is more, yet retains a strong sense of coziness, comfort and warmth.

CHANGING SPACES

The open-plan living space echoes the surrounding woodlands with stained timber cladding on the walls and ceiling, adding depth and character to the room. There are a number of versatile pieces of furniture in this space, from the dining table to the armchairs in front of the large panes of glass. This home challenges the preconceptions that interior layouts have to be fixed. The idea here is that the interior can be adjusted to meet the couple's changing needs.

FUNCTIONAL BEAUTY

The materials in this home have been carefully chosen to reflect Mette and Masahiro's lifestyle. For those who love to cook, a stainless-steel kitchen is not just hard-wearing and practical, but also valued for its attractive design-led look (previous spread). The high-gloss cabinets complement the other materials and are softened here with stone, glass and ceramic kitchenware.

WABI-SABI INFLUENCES

The entrance to the house reflects principles from Japanese design that complement Scandinavian elements (opposite). It is a minimal space that celebrates subtlety and restraint; only necessary items are kept out on show and everything else is hidden behind hemp and cotton indigo fabric panels. The tabletop is made of driftwood from the sea and a pair of handthrown vases celebrate the beauty of the natural world (above).

CHARRED WOOD
The exterior is clad in cedar boards charred using the
Japanese Shou Sugi Ban method that renders the
wood resistant to fire, rot and the effects of UV light
(this page). The house might be new but it is home
to many vintage treasures (opposite).

MONASTIC MOOD

The dark and moody micro-cement bathroom pays homage to both classic Scandinavian and Japanese design (above). Materials and objects have been used sparingly here to create a subtle, understated interior and the dark tones are cocooning. There are no windows at eye level but a skylight above the shower illuminates the space.

RESTFUL SPACES

Approached via a corridor paved in smooth pebbles, the master bedroom has been designed with wabi-sabi principles in mind, focusing on simplicity and the beauty of natural materials (here and opposite). The low bed is the focal point, giving this small room a sense of spaciousness. The window that's level with the floor is reminiscent of Scandi design principles and reveals a desire to connect to nature.

SOURCE LIST

DECORATIVE ACCESSORIES

AERENDE
aerende.co.uk
Timeless, rustic-style products for the home crafted by makers facing social challenges.

ARTISANNE
artisanne.co.uk
Fair trade traditional baskets handwoven in Senegal.

CENTURY GENERAL STORE
Montrose House
1–7 Montrose Terrace
Edinburgh EH7 5DJ
centurygeneralstore.com
Homewares, gifts, zero-waste products for the kitchen and bathroom, houseplants and handmade ceramics.

THE FUTURE KEPT
thefuturekept.com
Consciously crafted, responsibly and ethically sourced household linens, accessories and textiles for the home.

GRAIN AND KNOT
grainandknot.com
Tactile wooden kitchenware made from reclaimed timber.

KSM CANDLE CO
knitssoyandmetal.com
Natural, hand-poured soy candles, candle-making kits, room sprays, diffusers and incense, as well as natural beauty products

OUR LOVELY GOODS
ourlovelygoods.com
Natural wax candles, home scents, botanical skincare and a selection of raffia homewares made by talented artisans in Nigeria.

TANAKA SOAPS
https:tanaka.store
Plant-based soaps handcrafted using the traditional cold process method. Each bar uses key ingredients to calm, soothe and heal.

TEXTILES

JORD HOME
jordhome.com
A boutique rug store offering cotton, jute and wool rugs and natural hides from Sweden, Norway and Finland as well as Beni Ourain rugs from the Atlas Mountains.

SECRET LINEN STORE
secretlinenstore.com
Soft, laundered 100% linen bedding and accessories.

CERAMICS

DANTE CERAMICS
dantesceramics.com/
Simple, solid and understated handmade stoneware designed for everyday living.

NAKED CLAY CERAMICS
nakedclayceramics.com/
Tactile, minimal tableware and homeware in black stoneware and white porcelain.

TOAST
Toa.st
Stockists of hand-pressed Wonki Ware stoneware from South Africa as well as other pieces from studio ceramicists.

GREENERY AND FLOWERS

FOREST
Rear of 43 Lordship Lane,
London SE22 8EW
+44 (0)20 8693 6088
forest.london
Bring nature into your home with houseplants and cut flowers, which are natural mood enhancers and can improve air quality by filtering polluted air.

WORM LONDON
The Common Room,
Old Hill Street,
London N16 6NB
weareworm.com
Floral design studio producing creative seasonal arrangements.

LIGHTING

ORIGINAL BTC
The Design Centre
228 Chelsea Harbour Drive
London SW10 0XE
+44 (0)20 7351 2130
originalbtc.com
Clean-lined, timeless lighting, handmade in the UK.

TOM RAFFIELD
tomraffield.com
A lighting and furniture business belonging to one of the homeowners featured in this book, Tom Raffield. Tom and his team create contemporary lighting and steam-bent furniture and accessories that celebrate the strength, versatility and unique tones of sustainably sourced ash wood.

FURNITURE AND HOMEWARES

ALICE IN SCANDILAND
28 Fore Street
Lostwithiel
Cornwall PL220BL
Shop.aliceinscandiland.com
A Scandinavian-inspired Cornish lifestyle store offering modern and vintage pieces in simple retro shapes.

BAILEY'S
Whitecross Farm,
Bridstow
Ross-on-Wye HR9 6JU
+44 (0)1989 561931
baileyshome.com
A destination rustic and sustainable lifestyle and furniture store in a Monmouthshire valley.

DESIGN VINTAGE
Kingley Centre
Downs Road
West Stoke
Chichester PO18 9HJ
+44 (0)1243 573852
designvintage.co.uk
Modern and vintage furniture, rugs, lighting and homewares.

FERM LIVING
fermliving.com
Danish brand offering furniture, lighting, wallpaper, rugs and more.

GOODEE
goodeeworld.com
A global marketplace offering ethically made and transparently sourced products, from bed linen to wallpaper.

IGIGI
31 Western Road
Hove BN3 1AF
+44 (0)1273 775257
igigigeneralstore.com/
Beautiful linens, lighting, natural homewares and bespoke one-of-a-kind pieces and furniture.

JUNE
junehomesupply.com
Canadian lifestyle store offering worldwide shopping with an emphasis on interiors that support simple living.

HAY
hay.dk
Furniture for modern living, from sofas, furniture to lighting and more.

MADAM STOLZ
madamstoltz.dk
Lots of rustic textures, textiles, bamboo furniture and lighting.

NKUKU
Brockhills Barns
Harbertonford
Totnes
Devon TQ9 7PS
+44 (0)1803 465365
nkuku.com
Lifestyle products from furniture to tableware created by artisans using natural materials.

ROWEN AND WREN
rowenandwren.co.uk
Furniture, lighting and home and garden accessories with an emphasis on simplicity and sustainability.

SKAGERAK DENMARK
skagerak.dk/uk
Sustainable outdoor furniture with pared-down Nordic styling.

STRING
stringfurniture.com
A flexible shelving system designed by Nisse and Kajsa Strinning in 1949. Timeless, high-quality furniture with a Scandinavian design.

SKANDIUM
skandium.com
Modern and contemporary Scandinavian design.

TINE K HOME
tinekhome.com
Danish design brand that combines bohemian style with elegant simplicity.

WHITE FLOWER
FARMHOUSE
53995 Main Rd
Southold
NY 11971
United States
+1 631-765-2353
A beautiful mix of painted white and bleached pine vintage and repurposed furniture, linen textiles, vintage hardware and more.

PAINT

BAUWERK
Bauwerkcolour.co.uk
Modern lime paint using the finest pigments in a beautiful range of colours for both modern and traditional buildings.

DETALE COPENHAGEN
detalecph.com
This Danish company has devised a range of innovative and tactile wall surfaces, including coloured plaster and paint with a fabric-like finish.

KALKLITIR
kalklitir.com
Family-owned company specializing in natural paints and decorative art. This paint was used by some of our Swedish homeowners in the book.

FLOORS

DINESEN
dinesen.com
Solid and engineered planks for wooden flooring, panelling, ceiling and other design elements.

WAXED FLOORS
92 Battersea Rise
London SW11 6NS
+44 (0)20 7738 1620
waxedfloors.co.uk
Supplier of bespoke hardwood floors.

ART

PERNILLE GRØNKJÆR
TAATØ
nordiskrum.dk
Original artworks in nuanced Scandi shades created by one of the location owners featured in this book.

CURIOUS EGG
curiousegg.com
Carefully chosen artworks, expressive homewares and beautiful handmade objects for the home.

MRS MIGHETTO
mrsmighetto.com
Swedish brand creating whimsical, ethereal prints, wallpapers, bed linen, artworks and accessories especially for children's rooms.

HIGH STREET/ RETAIL CHAINS

ANTHROPOLOGIE
158 Regent St
London W1B 5SW
and branches
+44 (0)20 7529 9800
anthropologie.com
Bohemian-inspired furniture, textiles, homeware and accessories

H&M HOME
208 Regent Street
London W1B 5BD
hm.com
Affordable and well-designed pieces for every room in the house.

IKEA
ikea.com
Global Scandinavian furnishing brand with an emphasis on affordable design

FRENCH CONNECTION
HOME
55 Duke St
London W1K 5NR
+44 (0)20 7629 7766
frenchconnection.com
Lighting, linen bedding, ceramics and a limited selection of furniture with a relaxed rustic aesthetic

NEPTUNE
neptune.com
Timeless, stylish kitchens, furniture and homeware with destination lifestyle stores across the UK and Europe

COX & COX
coxandcox.co.uk
Lighting, furniture and decorative accessories for indoors and out with a relaxed Scandinavian feel

PICTURE CREDITS

All photography by Ben Edwards

1 The Hide in Cornwall, available for rent via Unique Homestays www.uniquehomestays.com; 2–3 The home of Mike Read and Kate Lawley, @mike_and_kate; 5 A. Hubble at Island Cottage, West Sussex and Paul Cashin Architects; 6 Architects and homeowners Mette Fredskild and Masahiro Katsume; 7 The home in Sussex of Lisa Brass of Design Vintage; 9 centre Architects and homeowners Mette Fredskild and Masahiro Katsume; 10 The home of Kay Prestney @kinship_creativedc; 11 above The family home of designers Tom and Danielle Raffield www.tomraffield.com; 11 below A. Hubble at Island Cottage, West Sussex and Paul Cashin Architects; 12–13 The home of @susliving in Denmark; 14 The home of Mike Read and Kate Lawley, @mike_and_kate; 15 The home of Anna Kubel in Sweden; 16 styled by Rebecca Lawson and Reena Simon; 17 above Interior stylist and graphic designer Pernille Grønkjær Taatø of Nordiskrum.dk in Denmark; 17 below The home of Kay Prestney @kinship_creativedc; 18 styled by Rebecca Lawson and Reena Simon; 18 below The home of stylist and set designer Elin Wallin of Studio Elwa in Sweden; 19 above The home of Anna Kubel in Sweden; 19 below The home of Kay Prestney @kinship_creativedc; 20 centre right The home in Sussex of Lisa Brass of Design Vintage; 21 above The home of stylist and set designer Elin Wallin of Studio Elwa in Sweden; 21 below The home of Mike Read and Kate Lawley, @mike_and_kate; 22 Architects and homeowners Mette Fredskild and Masahiro Katsume; 23 The home of stylist and set designer Elin Wallin of Studio Elwa in Sweden; 24 The home of Kay Prestney @kinship_creativedc; 25 left A. Hubble at Island Cottage, West Sussex and Paul Cashin Architects; 25 centre The home of Anna Kubel in Sweden; 25 right The home of Kay Prestney @kinship_creativedc; 26 left and centre The family home of designers Tom and Danielle Raffield www.tomraffield.com; 26 right The home of Anna Kubel in Sweden; 27 above left The Hide in Cornwall, available for rent via Unique Homestays www.uniquehomestays.com; 27 below The family home of designers Tom and Danielle Raffield www.tomraffield.com; 28 The home in Sussex of Lisa Brass of Design Vintage; 29 left A. Hubble at Island Cottage, West Sussex and Paul Cashin Architects; 29 centre The home in Sussex of Lisa Brass of Design Vintage; 29 right The home of Mike Read and Kate Lawley, @mike_and_kate; 30 The home of Anna Kubel in Sweden; 31 The home of @susliving in Denmark; 32 left The home in Sussex of Lisa Brass of Design Vintage; 32 centre The family home of designers Tom and Danielle Raffield www.tomraffield.com; 32 right styled by Rebecca Lawson and Reena Simon; 33 The home of stylist and set designer Elin Wallin of Studio Elwa in Sweden; 34 and 35 The home of Kay Prestney @kinship_creativedc; 36 Architects and homeowners Mette Fredskild and Masahiro Katsume; 37 left The home of @susliving in Denmark; 37 centre and left The Hide in Cornwall, available for rent via Unique Homestays www.uniquehomestays.com; 38 The family home of designers Tom and Danielle Raffield www.tomraffield.com; 39 The Hide in Cornwall, available for rent via Unique Homestays: www.uniquehomestays.com; 40 left The home of stylist and set designer Elin Wallin of Studio Elwa in Sweden; 40 below right The home of Kay Prestney @kinship_creativedc; 40–41 centre The family home of designers Tom and Danielle Raffield www.tomraffield.com ; 41 above and below A. Hubble at Island Cottage, West Sussex and Paul Cashin Architects; 42–53 The home of Mike Read and Kate Lawley, @mike_and_kate; 54–63 A. Hubble at Island Cottage, West Sussex and Paul Cashin Architects; 64–75 The home of Kay Prestney @kinship_creativedc; 76–85 The home in Sussex of Lisa Brass of Design Vintage; 86–95 The family home of designers Tom and Danielle Raffield www.tomraffield.com; 96–103 The Hide in Cornwall, available for rent via Unique Homestays www.uniquehomestays.com; 104–111 The home of stylist and set designer Elin Wallin of Studio Elwa in Sweden; 112–121 The home of Anna Kubel in Sweden; 122–131 Interior stylist and graphic designer Pernille Grønkjær Taatø of Nordiskrum.dk in Denmark; 132–141 The home of @susliving in Denmark; 142–153 Architects and homeowners Mette Fredskild and Masahiro Katsume; 155 The home of Kay Prestney @kinship_creativedc; 158 The home in Sussex of Lisa Brass of Design Vintage; 160 The home of Mike Read and Kate Lawley, @mike_and_kate.

BUSINESS CREDITS

DESIGN VINTAGE
An eclectic mix of vintage
loveliness, modern homewares,
gifts and accessories
The Old Barn
1 Kingley Centre
West Stoke
Chichester
West Sussex PO18 9HJ
T: +44 (0)1243 573852
info@designvintage.co.uk
www.designvintage.co.uk
IG: designvintageuk
*Pages 7, 20 centre right, 28, 29 centre,
32 left, 76–85, 158.*

**METTE FREDSKILD
ARCHITECT**
Oster Sogade 22
1357 Copenhagen K
Denmark
E: mette@mettefredskild.dk
www.mettefredskild.dk
Pages 6, 9 centre, 22, 36, 142–153.

**HUBBLE KITCHENS &
INTERIORS**
www.hubblekitchens.co.uk
IG: hubblekitchensinteriors
and
PAUL CASHIN ARCHITECTS
Suite 11 Talbot House
Staple Gardens
Winchester
Hampshire SO23 8SR
T: +44 (0)1962 807 077
paul@paulcashinarchitects.
co.uk
www.paulcashinarchitects.co.uk
IG: pca_architects
*Pages 5, 11, 25 left, 29 left, 41 above,
41 below, 54–63.*

**PERNILLE GRØNKJÆR
TAATØ**
Nordisk Rum
Skovvaenget 24A

DK-3100 Hornbaek
Denmark
T: +45 24428971
pernille@nordiskrum.dk
www.nordiskrum.dk
IG: nordiskrum
IG: nordiskrum_artwork
www.facebook.com/
nordiskrum.dk
www.pinterest.com/
nordiskrum/
Pages 17 above, 122–131.

ANNA KUBEL
Photographer, Interior stylist,
Content Creator
Stockholm
Sweden
annakubels@gmail.com
www.annakubel.com
IG: annakubel
*Pages 15, 19 above, 25 centre, 26
right, 30, 112–121.*

SUSAN MOGENSEN
IG: @susliving
Pages 12, 13, 31, 37 left, 132 – 141.

KAY PRESTNEY
IG: @kinship_creativedc
*Pages 10, 17 below, 19 below, 24, 25
right, 34, 35, 40 below right, 64–75,
155.*

TOM RAFFIELD
Handcrafted sustainable
wooden lighting, furniture and
accessories.
www.tomraffield.com
*Pages 11 above, 26 left, 26 centre, 27
below, 32 centre, 38, 40–41, 86–95.*

**MIKE READ AND
KATE LAWLEY**
IG: mike_and_kate
*Pages 2–3, 14, 21 below, 29 right,
42–53, 160.*

UNIQUE HOMESTAYS
The Hide in Cornwall is
for rent via Unique Homestays
T: +44 (0)1637 881183
www.uniquehomestays.com
*Pages 1, 27 above left, 37 centre, 37
left, 39, 96–103.*

ELIN WALLIN
www.studioelwa.se
IG: @studioelwa
*Pages 18 below, 21 above, 23, 33, 40
left, 104–111.*

INDEX

ACKNOWLEDGMENTS

Working on this book has been a dream from start to finish. Venturing across Scandinavia and the UK in search of the coziest homes, we have made memories that will last a lifetime. A huge thank you must go to all of the Scandi Rustic homeowners who welcomed us with kindness and generosity, letting us spend the day with them and sharing their stories. Our book is a credit to them and their incredible homes. Somehow, we managed to shoot and wrap up in Cornwall just a few days before Covid-19 hit the UK.

We spent our time in lockdown writing the book at our respective homes rather than (as originally planned) holed up together in a Scandi Rustic getaway, but it was an enjoyable experience nonetheless thanks to the brilliant team at RPS. A special thank you to Cindy, Annabel, Leslie, Jess and Megan for the opportunity.

Huge thanks must also go to our talented photographer Benjamin Edwards, who not only captured the most beautiful pictures but drove us everywhere on our grand adventure. And lastly thanks to our husbands Gareth and Matt, who stayed at home with our six kids and let us live the dream.